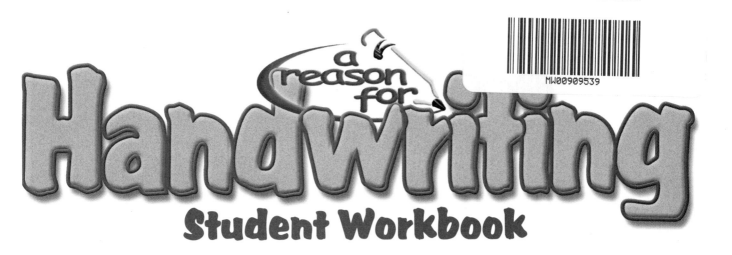

Handwriting

Student Workbook

Cursive

ISBN #0-936785-43-8

Published by Concerned Communications
700 East Granite • P.O. Box 1000 • Siloam Springs, AR 72761

Authors **Carol Ann Retzer, Eva Hoshino**
Publisher **Russ L. Potter, II**
Senior Editor **Bill Morelan**
Creative Director **Daniel Potter**
Copy Editor **Tricia Schnell Williams**
Proofreader **Trish Houston**
Illustrations **Rob Harrell**
Colorists **Josh & Aimee Ray**

Scripture translation selected for appropriate vocabulary level.
All verses are taken from *The Living Bible*, Tyndale House Publishers,
Wheaton, Illinois 60187. Used by permission.

printed on recycled paper

For more information about **A Reason For**® curricula,
write to the address above, call, or visit our website.

www.areasonfor.com
800.447.4332

Please, Don't Be A Copycat!

Copy machines are wonderful inventions, but did you know that it's ILLEGAL to reproduce copyrighted material?

Years of work and thousands of dollars have gone into developing the materials in this book. Only your Christian integrity can help us avoid unnecessary price increases due to unauthorized copying. (In most cases purchasing the material is less expensive than copying anyway!)

So please, don't yield to the temptation to "run off a few copies." It's not cost effective, and it's ILLEGAL as well!

For Parents & Teachers

Don't Settle for HALF a Curriculum!

A Reason For® Handwriting Student Workbooks integrate faith and learning by featuring lessons based on Scripture verses, and built-in opportunities for sharing God's Word with others.

But the **A Reason For®** Handwriting curriculum offers much, much more!

Every grade level includes a comprehensive Teacher Guidebook full of essential instructions, helpful tips, and teacher-tested techniques to help you make the most of your handwriting practice.

Key instructional information in the Teacher Guidebook includes:

- The Suggested Weekly Schedule
- Daily Lesson Plans
- Tips for Teaching Cursive Handwriting
- Techniques for Grading

Plus *every* Teacher Guidebook includes a wealth of teacher-tested tips and enrichment ideas:

- A Comprehensive Skills Index
- Extended Activities
- Ways to Share Border Sheets
- Letter Formation Charts
- Tips for Proper Positioning
- Letter Group Charts
- Vocabulary Lists
- Common Handwriting Problems
- Black Line Masters

To order the **A Reason For®** Handwriting Teacher Guidebook
that goes with this Student Workbook, contact your curriculum supplier or call:

800.447.4332

Or write to:
Concerned Communications
P.O. Box 1000
Siloam Springs, AR 72761

Just For Kids!

Welcome to
A Reason For© Handwriting

This year you'll learn to write better. . . share God's Word. . .and have FUN!

Each week you'll practice letters and groups of letters from a different Scripture verse. Then you'll write the entire verse on practice paper. At the end of each week you'll pick a **Scripture Border Sheet** from the back of your workbook, write

Quentin

Isabelle

Devin

the verse in your very best handwriting, and use your creative talents to color and decorate it. Now comes the FUN part.

You can share God's Word by giving people your finished Scripture Border Sheets! You can take them to nursing homes, share them with friends, make placemats for your kitchen table, mail them to someone who isn't feeling well. . . you get the idea.

And sharing God's Word with others gives you the very best reason for improving your handwriting!

Handwriting Friends

Throughout this book, you'll see illustrations of kids just like you caring, sharing, working, and learning. Be sure to watch for these new friends!

Nekomi

Oscar

Kindra

Kenichi

Hayley

Be A Five Star Student!

Do you want your writing to look its very best? Here are the five basic areas you should consider when evaluating your handwriting form:

Alignment
Each letter should sit *on* the line, not above or below it.

Slant
The letter slant should be uniform and consistent. (To help you determine direction, draw a line straight down the middle of each letter in a sentence.)

Size
Capital letters are all one full space tall. The lowercase letters *b, d, f, h, k, l,* and *t* are also one space tall. All other lowercase letters are half a space tall. Also, any letter that goes below the line should extend for half a space.

Shape
Letters should be consistent and easy to read. Minor differences from the model are okay, but all your letters must be formed with the proper strokes to avoid developing bad habits.

Spacing
Letters should be clearly identifiable. They should not run into each other, or be too far apart. Each word should be separated from the next word. Remember, a little more space is needed between sentences than between words.

Follow these guidelines, focusing on consistency and quality, and you'll be a **Five Star** student!

The following practice sentence contains all the letters of the alphabet:

God created the zebras and foxes to walk, jump, and hide very quickly.

To The Teacher

Before beginning instruction, please review the
Weekly Lesson Format (Teacher Guidebook, page 6).

Here you will find detailed directions for implementing
the 5-day format, as well as suggestions for using the
Scripture Border Sheets.

Careful review of this material at the start of the school year
will greatly enhance the effectiveness of this curriculum.

Name _____

TIP OF THE WEEK

This year, focus on working carefully through each
handwriting lesson. Rushing only creates bad habits! Using
the **Five Star** evaluation (page 6) can help you become a better writer.

Day One Practice the following letters and words from this week's Scripture.

Aa   Aa   Aa a a   Aa   Aa   Aa

All   all   all   all   all

all   all   all   all

that   that   that   that

that

day

Day Two Continue practicing letters and words from this week's Scripture.

Ii

I'll

praise

done

9

Day Three Continue practicing letters and words from this week's Scripture.

Gg

God

long

honor

Day Four Write this week's Scripture verse on a sheet of practice paper.

All day long I'll praise and honor You, Oh God, for all that You have done for me.

Psalm 71:8

FOR DISCUSSION

What are some ways that you can praise or honor God? Make a list of some blessings that God has given you.

Tip of the week

Make certain your lowercase oval letters
(a, c, d, g, o, q) touch both lines. Also, check the
shape of each letter to make sure it's closed — except the c, of course!

Day One Practice the following letters and words from this week's Scripture.

Oo Oo Oo Oo Oo Oo Oo Oo Oo

Overlook Overlook Overlook

through through through

eyes eyes eyes eyes eyes

Day Two Continue practicing letters and words from this week's Scripture.

L l

Lord

youthful

love

Day Three Continue practicing letters and words from this week's Scripture.

Uu

forgiveness

everlasting

sins

Day Four Write this week's Scripture verse on a sheet of practice paper.

Overlook my youthful sins, Oh, Lord! Look at me instead through eyes of mercy and forgiveness, through eyes of everlasting love and kindness.

Psalm 25:6,7

FOR DISCUSSION

Give an example of God's love and kindness. What are some ways you can share God's love with others?

Name _____

TIP OF THE WEEK

Notice how much easier it is to write when you
sit up straight with both feet flat on the floor. Also, check to
make sure your paper is going the same direction as your writing arm.

①

Day One Practice the following letters and words from this week's Scripture.

Cc

Create

clean

new

②

Day Two Continue practicing letters and words from this week's Scripture.

Dd

God

filled

right

Day Three Continue practicing letters and words from this week's Scripture.

Ss

desires

thoughts

willing

Day Four Write this week's Scripture verse on a sheet of practice paper. ④

Create in me a new, clean heart, Oh God, filled with clean thoughts and right desires... make me willing to obey You.

Psalm 51:10,12

FOR DISCUSSION

Rewrite this verse in your own words, making it into a personal commitment. Why not share it with God tonight when you pray?

TIP OF THE WEEK

There are many different kinds of punctuation
in this week's Scripture. Watch for the period, elipses,
and quotation marks. What other type of puncuation can you find?

Day One   Practice the following letters and words from this week's Scripture.

Ee

Every

tell

evening

Day Two   Continue practicing letters and words from this week's Scripture.

Kk

kindness

rejoice

morning

Yy

Thank You

joy

sing

Every morning tell Him,
"Thank You for Your kindness,"
and every evening rejoice in all
His faithfulness...You have done so
much for me...I sing for joy.
Psalm 92:2,4

FOR DISCUSSION

How much time do you spend talking to your best friend each day? Be sure to take some special time to talk to God each day, too!

TIP OF THE WEEK

This Scripture contains the tail letters *f*, *g*, *j*, and *y*.
Write them on practice paper (in groups of three) to work on
your connecting strokes. Make certain the tails touch the bottom line.

Day One   Practice the following letters and words from this week's Scripture.

Nn

near

thinking

never

Day Two   Continue practicing letters and words from this week's Scripture.

Mm

stumble

am

Psalm

F f

fall

filled

always

I am always thinking of the
Lord; and because He is so near,
I never need to stumble or to fall.
Heart, body, and soul are filled
with joy.

Psalm 16:8,9

FOR DISCUSSION

List some ways that "thinking of the Lord"
can make a person joyful. How can this
affect your attitude when things go wrong?

Name _____

📚 TIP OF THE WEEK

This week's capital letters (*J*, *I*, and *Q*) all begin with
the upswing. It takes practice to write them all with the same
slant. Check to see how much better you're doing by the end of the week.

Day One Practice the following letters and words from this week's Scripture.

Jj

Just

tell

what

Day Two Continue practicing letters and words from this week's Scripture.

Ii

I

will

live

Q q

quickly

wholeheartedly

long

Day Four   Write this week's Scripture verse on a sheet of practice paper.

Just tell me what to do and I will do it, Lord. As long as I live I'll wholeheartedly obey.

Psalm 119:33, 34

FOR DISCUSSION

How does showing obedience to God relate to your relationship with your parents? (See Exodus 20:12.) List some ways you can show this kind of obedience.

Name _____

TIP OF THE WEEK

Many letters are never delivered because the name
and address are unreadable. Don't let it happen to you!
Watch the size and shape of your letters as you write this week.

Day One Practice the following letters and words from this week's Scripture.

Bb

Be

delighted

give

Day Two Continue practicing letters and words from this week's Scripture.

It

Then

heart's

Trust

Cc

Commit

desires

all

Be delighted with the Lord.
Then He will give you all your
heart's desires. Commit everything
you do to the Lord. Trust Him to
help you do it and He will.

Psalm 37:4,5

FOR DISCUSSION

What does "commit" mean in this Scripture verse?
Look at James 1:5. How is it similiar to the
last half of this verse.

Name _____

TIP OF THE WEEK

The forward oval capitals B, P, and R
all begin the same way. As you practice them
this week, watch for their similarities and differences.

Day One Practice the following letters and words from this week's Scripture.

P p

Pour

help

people

Day Two Continue practicing letters and words from this week's Scripture.

H h

He

Him

Oh

Day Three — Continue practicing letters and words from this week's Scripture.

Oo

before

longings

out

Day Four — Write this week's Scripture verse on a sheet of practice paper.

Oh my people, trust Him all the time. Pour out your longings before Him, for He can help!

Psalm 62:8

FOR DISCUSSION

Does God always answer our prayers with "yes"?
What other answers might God give? Why?
How does "trust" fit into this picture?

Name _____

TIP OF THE WEEK

Work on your writing slant this week. You can check
to see if the slant is consistent by drawing a line (top to bottom)
through each letter. If your slant is correct, the lines will be parallel.

Day One Practice the following letters and words from this week's Scripture.

Rr

Righteousness

throne

strong

Day Two Continue practicing letters and words from this week's Scripture.

Uu

founded

one

two

Jj

Justice

joyful

pillars

Day Four   Write this week's Scripture verse on a sheet of practice paper.

Your throne is founded on two
strong pillars — the one is Justice
and the other Righteousness.

Psalm 89:14

JUSTICE

RIGHTEOUSNESS

FOR DISCUSSION

Look up the definitions for "justice" and
"righteousness." How are they similar?
How are they different?

Name _____

TIP OF THE WEEK

The canestroke capital letters are *H, K, M, N, U,*
V, W, X, Y. Although they all begin the same, they are
very different. Can you match the letters that are most similar?

Day One Practice the following letters and words from this week's Scripture.

Mm

My

enemy

where

Day Two Continue practicing letters and words from this week's Scripture.

Ee

protection

success

refuge

Day Three   Continue practicing letters and words from this week's Scripture.

A a

reach

alone

Rock

Day Four   Write this week's Scripture verse on a sheet of practice paper.

My protection and success come from God alone. He is my refuge, a Rock where no enemy can reach me.

Psalm 62:7

FOR DISCUSSION
What does the word "refuge" mean in this verse. List some ways that God protects us every day.

Name_____

TIP OF THE WEEK

For speed and smoothness in writing, remember to
cross the *x* and *t* after the word is written. (This week's word
except gives you double practice!) Be sure the *t* touches the top line.

Day One Practice the following letters and words from this week's Scripture.

Nn

Nothing

think

than

Day Two Continue practicing letters and words from this week's Scripture.

Xx

except

guide

are

Ss

enemies

constant

wiser

Day Four Write this week's Scripture verse on a sheet of practice paper.

Nothing is perfect except Your words. Oh, how I love them. I think about them all day long. They make me wiser than my enemies, because they are my constant guide.

Psalm 119:96-98

FOR DISCUSSION

What kind of wisdom can be found in God's Word? List at least three principles from Scripture that apply to your daily life.

If you've ever ridden a skateboard, you know how
important it is to stay balanced. This week, make certain
your letters are balanced on the lines. This is called letter alignment.

Day One Practice the following letters and words from this week's Scripture.

Hh

How

hands

shall

Day Two Continue practicing letters and words from this week's Scripture.

Rr

praise

prayer

last

Ff

lifting

fully

satisfied

Day Four Write this week's Scripture verse on a sheet of practice paper.

How I praise you! I will bless you as long as I live, lifting up my hands to you in prayer. At last I shall be fully satisfied; I will praise you with great joy.
Psalm 63:3-5

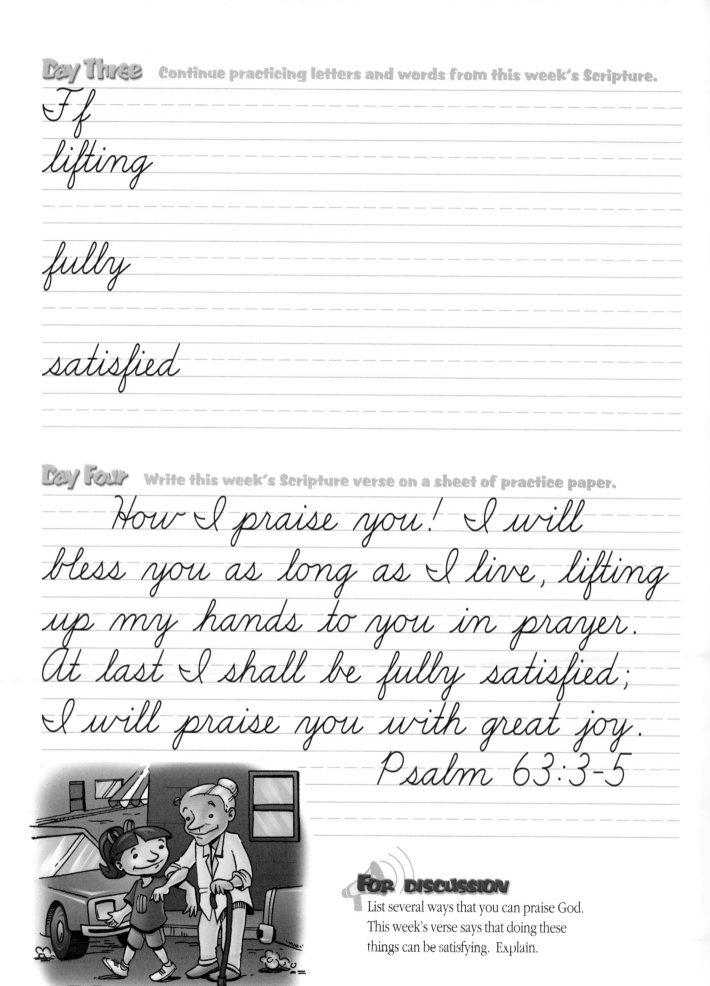

FOR DISCUSSION

List several ways that you can praise God. This week's verse says that doing these things can be satisfying. Explain.

TIP OF THE WEEK

The lowercase *b*, *o*, *v*, and *w* have a connecting
bridgestroke that does not dip to the line. Written correctly,
this stroke helps prevent misreading of words. Practice it carefully.

Day One   Practice the following letters and words from this week's Scripture.

Kk

Keep

every

undeserving

Day Two   Continue practicing letters and words from this week's Scripture.

Ww

wrong

laws

have

Bb

obey

chosen

far

Day Four Write this week's Scripture verse on a sheet of practice paper.

Keep me far from every
wrong; help me, undeserving as
I am, to obey Your laws, for I
have chosen to do right.

Psalm 119:29, 30

FOR DISCUSSION

Some of God's laws are similar to the laws
where we live. Give some examples.
Why is it important to obey laws?

Lesson 14

TIP OF THE WEEK

As you practice the word *quality* this week,
remember that God wants you to always do your very
best. What two letters in the word *quality* always go together?

Day One Practice the following letters and words from this week's Scripture.

Uu

Unless

useless

builds

Day Two Continue practicing letters and words from this week's Scripture.

Qq

quality

work

house

Ii

builders'

sentries

city

Day Four   Write this week's Scripture verse on a sheet of practice paper.

Unless the Lord builds a house,
the builders' work is useless.
Unless the Lord protects a city,
sentries do no good.

Psalm 127:1

FOR DISCUSSION

What does this verse means when it says, "Unless the Lord builds a house, the builders work is useless"? Does God build houses? Explain.

TIP OF THE WEEK

Remember, good posture makes a difference in
the quality of your writing. For the best results, make certain
you are sitting up straight, and that your feet are both flat on the floor.

Day One Practice the following letters and words from this week's Scripture.

Vv

Very

vastness

earth

Day Two Continue practicing letters and words from this week's Scripture.

Gg

Glory

living

sea

Oo

shout

on

roar

Day Four   Write this week's Scripture verse on a sheet of practice paper.

Let the sea in all its vastness roar with praise! Let the earth and all those living on it shout, "Glory to the Lord."

Psalm 98:7

FOR DISCUSSION

Compare this verse to Proverbs 6:6. What other lessons might we learn from watching nature?

Name _____

TIP OF THE WEEK

Y, J, and *Z* are the only capital tail letters.
For extra practice, copy them onto practice paper, making sure their
tails extend to the bottom line. What do these letters have in common with the *E* and *K*?

Day One   Practice the following letters and words from this week's Scripture.

Yy

Your

sky

vast

Day Two   Continue practicing letters and words from this week's Scripture.

Ee

love

heavens

faithfulness

Kk

kindness

skies

higher

Day Four   Write this week's Scripture verse on a sheet of practice paper.

Your kindness and love are
as vast as the heavens. Your
faithfulness is higher than the
skies.

Psalm 57:10

FOR DISCUSSION

God says His love is "as vast as the heavens." How would
you describe your love for God? How about your
parents? your friends? your enemies?

TIP OF THE WEEK

Pay close attention to your letter
spacing. If your letters are too close together,
then theywillbehardtoread. See what we mean?

Day One Practice the following letters and words from this week's Scripture.

Ww

What

who

How

Day Two Continue practicing letters and words from this week's Scripture.

Pp

perfect

prove

promises

Nn

behind

hides

true

What a God He is! How perfect in every way! All His promises prove true. He is a shield for everyone who hides behind Him.
Psalm 18:30

FOR DISCUSSION

What does this verse mean when it says God is our shield? List some ways that your relationship with God can shield you from evil.

TIP OF THE WEEK

This week we have two bonus words.
To discover them, look up Psalm 64:9. Here's a hint:
This verse should help you *realize* how *amazing* God is!

Day One   Practice the following letters and words from this week's Scripture.

Xx

exceeding

will

Oh

Day Two   Continue practicing letters and words from this week's Scripture.

Zz

realize

amazing

my

Rr

There

altar

harp

There I will go to the altar of God my exceeding joy, and praise Him with my harp. Oh God— my God!

Psalm 43:4

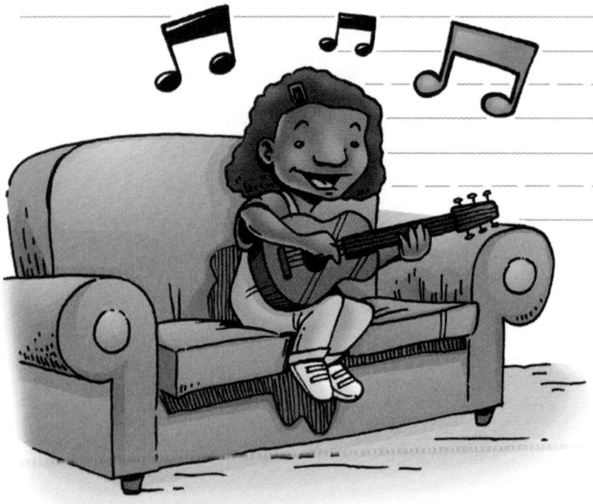

FOR DISCUSSION

There are many ways we can praise God.
Make a list of some of your favorites.
Now compare this list with a friend's.

Lesson 19

TIP OF THE WEEK

Time to be a **Five Star** student! As you write
your letters this week, pay close attention to all five areas.
Trade papers with a classmate, then point out each other's best words.

Day One   Practice the following letters and words from this week's Scripture.

Dd

Don't

stouthearted

Wait

Day Two   Continue practicing letters and words from this week's Scripture.

Bb

brave

Yes

save

Mm

impatient

come

courageous

Day Four   Write this week's Scripture verse on a sheet of practice paper.

Don't be impatient. Wait for the Lord, and He will come and save you! Be brave, stouthearted and courageous. Yes, wait and He will help you.

Psalm 27:14

FOR DISCUSSION

The words brave and courageous usually refer to action. Why does this verse use these words for waiting? Why is waiting so hard sometimes?

Name _____

Tip of the week

There are lots of lowercase tall letters this week
(*b*, *d*, *f*, *h*, *k*, *l*, and *t*). Some have loops, and some do not.
Make certain you practice them correctly, and that all tall letters touch the top line.

Day One Practice the following letters and words from this week's Scripture.

L l

Let

lives

bless

Day Two Continue practicing letters and words from this week's Scripture.

H h

His

holds

hands

A a

And

praises

path

Let everyone bless God and
sing His praises, for He holds our
lives in His hands. And He holds
our feet to the path.

Psalm 66:8,9

FOR DISCUSSION

What do you think the word "path"
means in this verse? List some ways that a
relationship with God keeps us on this path.

TIP OF THE WEEK

Focus on the dotted letters *j* and *i* this week.

Think of five words that contain either *j* or *i* and write them

on practice paper. Remember to dot these letters after you finish the word.

Day One   Practice the following letters and words from this week's Scripture.

Gg

God's

gold

dripping

Day Two   Continue practicing letters and words from this week's Scripture.

Jj

just

honeycomb

desirable

It

They

sweeter

eternal

Day Four   Write this week's Scripture verse on a sheet of practice paper.

God's laws are pure, eternal, just. They are more desirable than gold. They are sweeter than honey dripping from a honeycomb.

Psalm 19:9,10

FOR DISCUSSION

How does your relationship with God affect on how you relate to His laws? How can a law be "sweet?"

Tip of the week

When you drive a car, you must keep all four
tires on the road. When you write a word, you must keep
all the letters on the line. Pay close attention to letter alignment this week.

Day One Practice the following letters and words from this week's Scripture.

Ss

Show

should

gives

Day Two Continue practicing letters and words from this week's Scripture.

Vv

salvation

have

Lead

Day Three   Continue practicing letters and words from this week's Scripture.

Xx

except

point

road

Day Four   Write this week's Scripture verse on a sheet of practice paper.

Show me the path where I should go, Oh Lord; point out the right road for me to walk. Lead me; teach me; for You are the God Who gives me salvation. I have no hope except in you.
Psalm 25:4,5

FOR DISCUSSION

Scripture and nature are sometimes referred to as "God's two books." How does God use these things to teach us? Give some examples.

Lesson 23

TIP OF THE WEEK

This week each capital letter begins with a different
stroke. Imagine someone who has never written before.
How would you tell them how to write each of these capital letters?

Day One Practice the following letters and words from this week's Scripture.

Qq

Quick

quietly

answer

Day Two Continue practicing letters and words from this week's Scripture.

Yy

You

prayed

cry

L l

Listen

help

when

Quick, Lord, answer me – for I have prayed. Listen when I cry to You for help!

Psalm 141:1

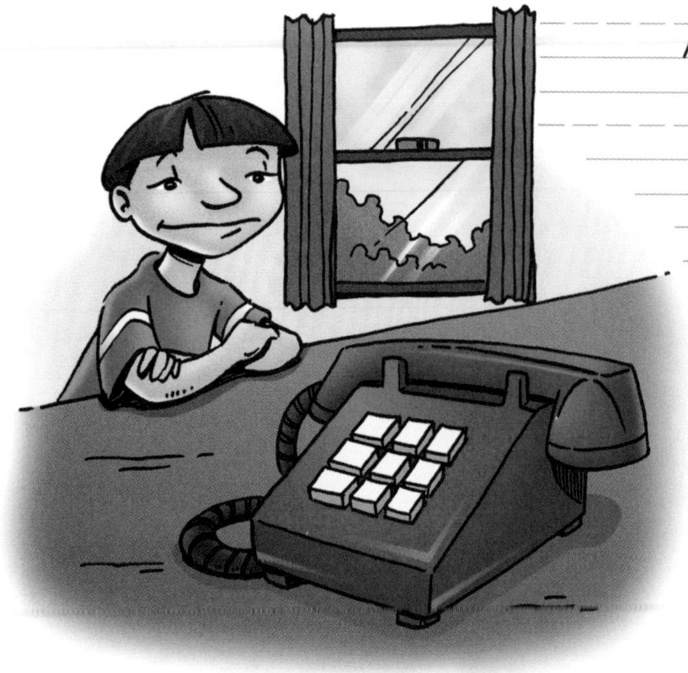

FOR DISCUSSION

Describe an answer to prayer that happened to you or someone you know. What kind of other answers might God use?

Name _____

TIP OF THE WEEK

If you have trouble holding your hand steady as you write,
you may be holding your pencil too tightly. Focus on the *un*
and *um* combinations this week, as well as the lowercase overstroke letters.

Day One Practice the following letters and words from this week's Scripture.

Zz

Zion

Those

as

Day Two Continue practicing letters and words from this week's Scripture.

Uu

trust

unmoved

any

Day Three Continue practicing letters and words from this week's Scripture.

Mm

Mount

circumstance

steady

Day Four Write this week's Scripture verse on a sheet of practice paper.

Those who trust in the Lord are steady as Mount Zion, unmoved by any circumstance.

Psalm 125:1

FOR DISCUSSION

List some unexpected circumstances that you (or someone you know) has had to face. How can trusting God help us in such situations?

Lesson 25

TIP OF THE WEEK

As you practice the boatstroke capital $\mathcal{F}$,
think of other capital letters that end with the same stroke.
Also, notice that boatstoke capitals never connect to the rest of the word.

Day One Practice the following letters and words from this week's Scripture.

Ff

Friendship

for

reserved

Day Two Continue practicing letters and words from this week's Scripture.

Ww

With

reverence

alone

Cc

secrets

shares

promises

Day Four   Write this week's Scripture verse on a sheet of practice paper.

Friendship with God is
reserved for those who reverence
Him. With them alone He shares
the secrets of His promises.
                              Psalm 25:14

FOR DISCUSSION

Why would God reserve his "secrets" for those
who reverence Him? List some ways that we
can show reverence for God.

TIP OF THE WEEK

There are a couple of tricky combinations
this week. Remember that the lowercase *r* and *s*
are not rounded, but are always written with distinct, sharp points.

Day One Practice the following letters and words from this week's Scripture.

Tt

Trust

others

instead

Day Two Continue practicing letters and words from this week's Scripture.

Nn

kind

feeding

land

Rr

here

prosper

safely

Day Four   Write this week's Scripture verse on a sheet of practice paper.

Trust in the Lord instead.
Be kind and good to others; then
you will live safely here in the
land and prosper, feeding in
safety.

Psalm 37:3

4 FOOD GROUPS

ACTIVITY BOARD

FOR DISCUSSION
List several ways you can show kindness to each
of the following: your parents, your friends,
your classmates, and the elderly.

Name _____

TIP OF THE WEEK

Remember, your name is the most important
word you write! Always write it with care. (That way,
you will be sure to get credit for all those great papers you're turning in!)

Day One Practice the following letters and words from this week's Scripture.

Bb

But

been

about

Day Two Continue practicing letters and words from this week's Scripture.

Yy

mercy

safety

high

Day Three Continue practicing letters and words from this week's Scripture.

Dd

distress

power

tower

Day Four Write this week's Scripture verse on a sheet of practice paper.

But as for me, I will sing each morning about Your power and mercy. For You have been my high tower of refuge, a place of safety in the day of my distress.
Psalm 59:16

FOR DISCUSSION

What does this verse mean when it says God is our "high tower of refuge"? Look at your list from Lesson 10. What else would you add?

Name _____

📚 **TIP OF THE WEEK**

As you write your *e*'s and *i*'s this week, notice that
one needs a small loop, and the other doesn't. These two letters
create many spelling errors when they are not written carefully and correctly.

Day One Practice the following letters and words from this week's Scripture.

Jj

Jehovah

Himself

defender

Day Two Continue practicing letters and words from this week's Scripture.

Ii

evil

night

caring

Pp

Psalm

protects

preserves

Day Four Write this week's Scripture verse on a sheet of practice paper.

Jehovah Himself is caring for you! He is your defender. He protects you day and night. He keeps you from all evil, and preserves your life.

Psalm 121:5-7

FOR DISCUSSION

Continue the discussion of God's protection from last week. Share your list with a classmate. How are they similar? How are they different?

TIP OF THE WEEK

If your hand gets tired from writing, you may be holding
your pencil too tightly! Also, to keep your slant consistent,
make certain your paper is at the same angle as your writing arm.

Day One Practice the following letters and words from this week's Scripture.

Cc

Come

clap

triumphant

Day Two Continue practicing letters and words from this week's Scripture.

Ss

Shout

words

awesome

Kk

King

beyond

great

Day Four   Write this week's Scripture verse on a sheet of practice paper.

Come, everyone, and clap for joy!
Shout triumphant praises to the
Lord! For the Lord, the God above
all gods, is awesome beyond words;
He is the great King of all the earth.
Psalm 47:1,2

FOR DISCUSSION
How do people react when their team makes
a touchdown? In what way does this relate
to this week's verse?

Watch your lowercase letters this week. Make certain
your tall letters touch the top line; your tail letters touch
the lower line; and your oval letters fill the space completely.

Day One Practice the following letters and words from this week's Scripture.

Ww

Who

with

stand

Day Two Continue practicing letters and words from this week's Scripture.

Oo

Only

dishonesty

hearts

L l

Lord

lying

practice

Who may stand before the Lord? Only those with pure hands and hearts, who do not practice dishonesty and lying.
Psalm 24:3,4

FOR DISCUSSION

What kinds of problems are created by telling lies? Are there other ways to be dishonest besides lying? Explain.

Name _____

TIP OF THE WEEK

The oval capital letters C and E start with the same stroke, which begins just below the top line. Can you think of some words describing the characteristics of God that begin with these two letters?

Day One Practice the following letters and words from this week's Scripture.

Ff

For

filled

earth

Day Two Continue practicing letters and words from this week's Scripture.

Ee

tender

everything

does

Day Three
Continue practicing letters and words from this week's Scripture.

Hh

whatever

worthy

right

Day Four
Write this week's Scripture verse on a sheet of practice paper.

For all God's words are right,
and everything He does is worthy
of our trust. He loves whatever is
just and good; the earth is filled
with His tender love.

Psalm 33:4,5

FOR DISCUSSION

To really trust someone, you have to get to know them, and they have to be trustworthy. How does that relate to this verse?

Time for a final **Five Star** evaluation. Compare your
writing from the beginning of the year with this lesson. Remember,
with God's help, you can use your writing to make a difference in the world!

Day One Practice the following letters and words from this week's Scripture.

Tt

Teach

they

them

Day Two Continue practicing letters and words from this week's Scripture.

Zz

recognize

number

few

Dd

spend

days

should

Day Four Write this week's Scripture verse on a sheet of practice paper.

Teach us to number our days and recognize how few they are; help us to spend them as we should.

Psalm 90:12

FOR DISCUSSION

List some good ways to spend time each day. In what way are these different from wasteful activities? How can you apply these ideas this summer?

To The Teacher

The following pages are for use on Day 5 of the
Weekly Lesson Format (Teacher Guidebook, page 6).

These **Scripture Border Sheets** not only provide a
significant outreach component, but a strong
motivational tool as well.

This section contains 35 **Scripture Border Sheets** —
one per lesson, plus an extra, plus two blanks (pages 141
and 143) that allow for student-designed artwork.

For creative ways to use the **Scripture Border Sheets**
see "Ways to Share" (Teacher Guidebook, page 8).

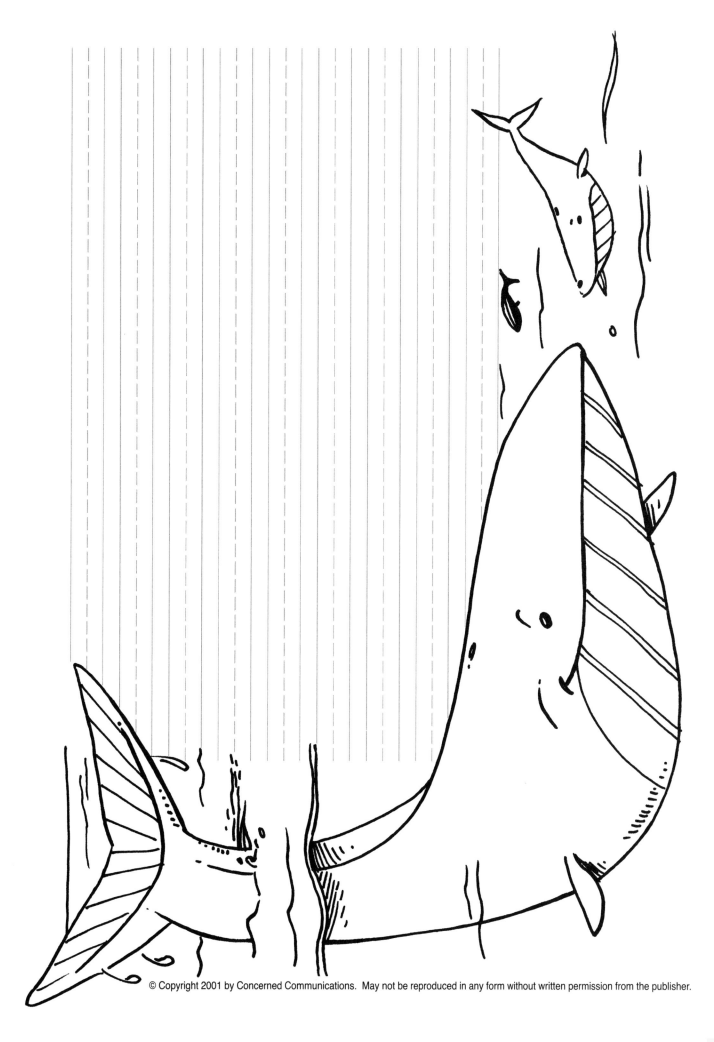

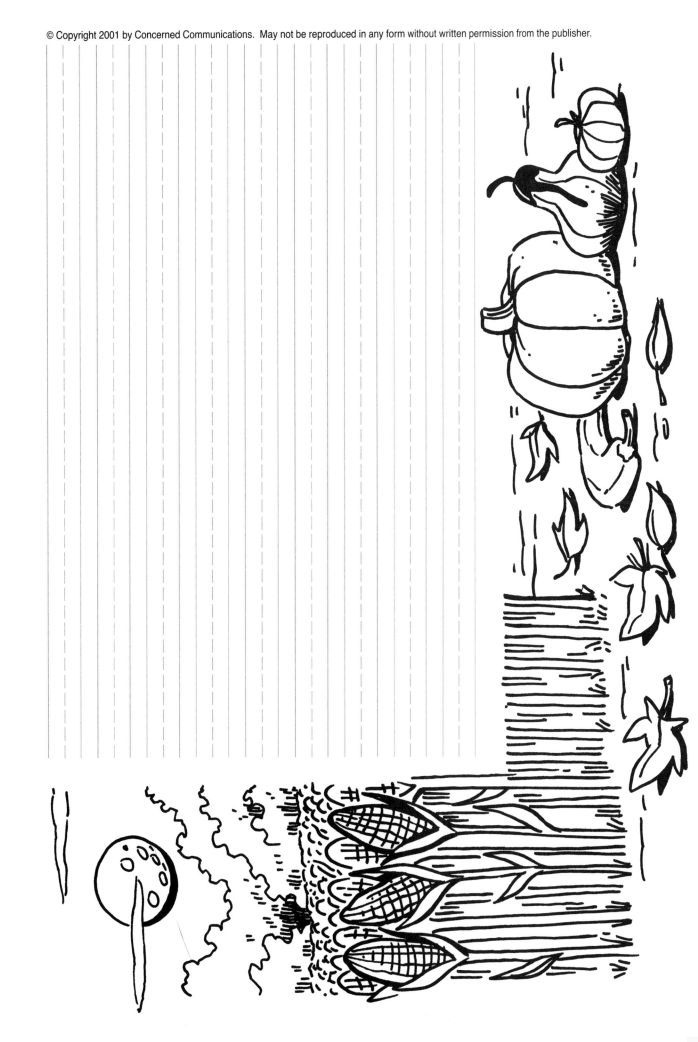

116

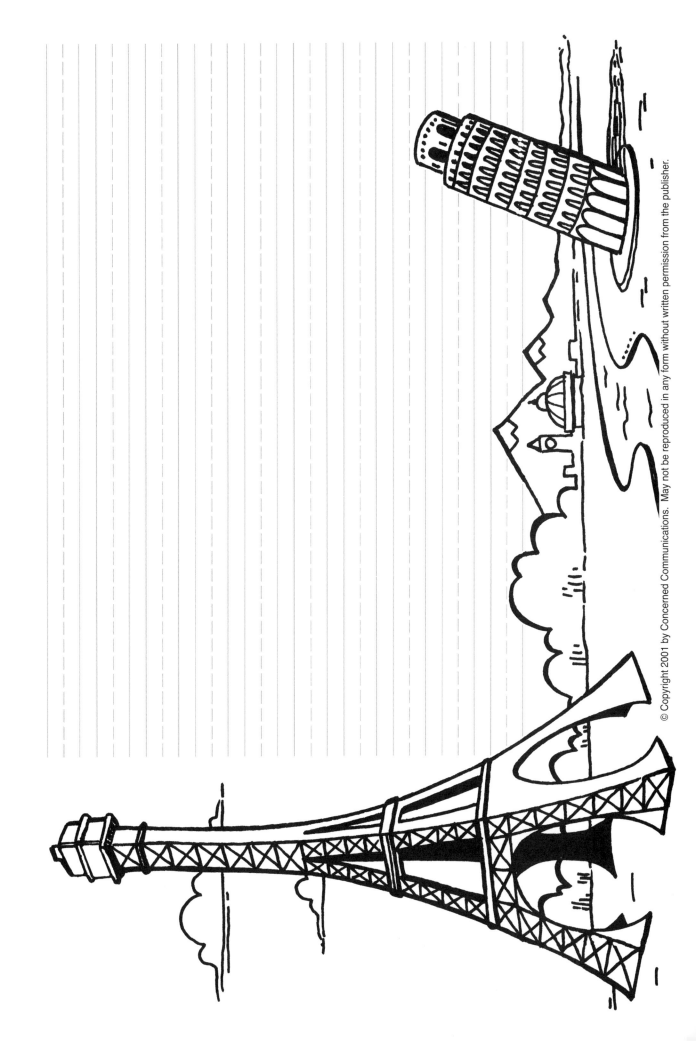

134

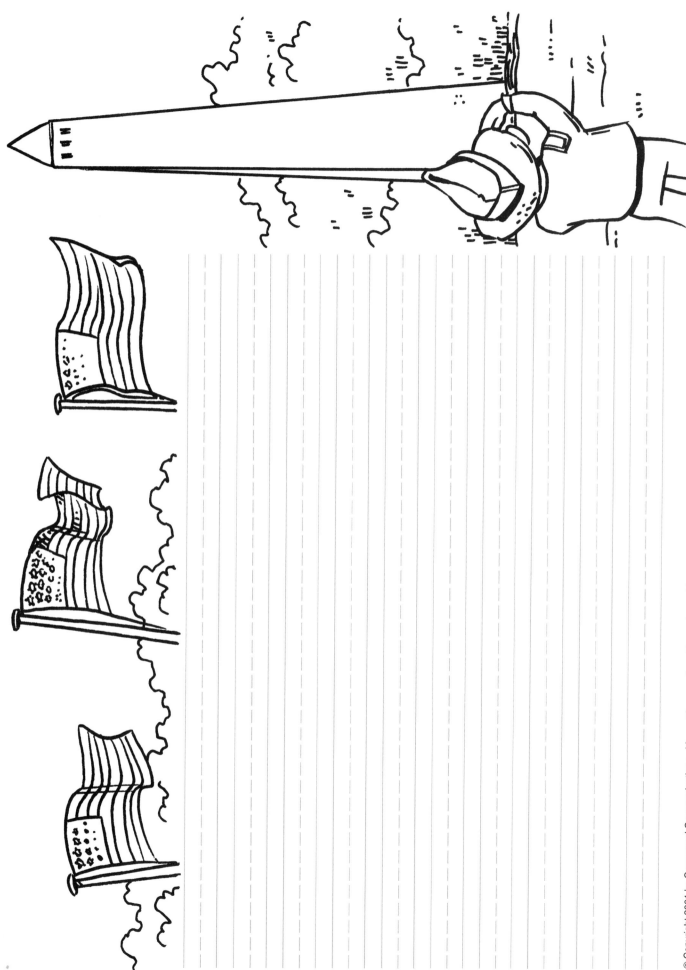